frame>by>frame
asian

frame>by>frame
asian

a visual step-by-step cookbook

First published in 2010
LOVE FOOD is an imprint of Parragon Books Ltd

Parragon
Queen Street House
4 Queen Street
Bath BA1 1HE, UK

ISBN: 978-1-4075-9092-9

Printed in China

Designed by Talking Design
Photography by Mike Cooper
Home economy by Lincoln Jefferson
New recipes by Christine France
Introduction by Linda Doeser

Notes for the Reader
This book uses imperial, metric, and US cup measurements. Follow the same units of measurement throughout; do not mix imperial and metric. All spoon measurements are level: teaspoons are assumed to be 5 ml, and tablespoons are assumed to be 15 ml. Unless otherwise stated, milk is assumed to be whole, eggs and individual vegetables such as potatoes are medium, and pepper is freshly ground black pepper.

The times given are an approximate guide only. Preparation times differ according to the techniques used by different people and the cooking times may also vary from those given as a result of the type of oven used. Optional ingredients, variations or serving suggestions have not been included in the calculations.

Recipes using raw or very lightly cooked eggs, fish, meat, or poultry should be avoided by infants, the elderly, pregnant women, convalescents, and anyone with a chronic illness. Pregnant and breast-feeding women are advised to avoid eating peanuts and peanut products. Sufferers from nut allergies should be aware that some of the prepared ingredients used in the recipes in this book may contain nuts. Always check the packaging before use.

Although sushi is traditionally made using both raw and cooked fish, all of the sushi recipes in this book can be made with cooked fish. If you are using raw fish, then ensure that it is as fresh as possible, has been bought from a reputable supplier selling sushi- or sashimi-grade fish, and has been stored at a low temperature in a refrigerator until serving. Ensure that fish is prepared using clean utensils.

contents

introduction

This superlative cookbook with its wealth of lovely and tremendously useful photographs will prove to be an invaluable and delightful addition to any cook's bookshelf. The recipes are clear, easy to follow, beautifully illustrated, wonderfully tasty, and truly authentic, so whatever your level of expertise in the kitchen you are virtually guaranteed success every time.

Every recipe starts with a photograph of all the ingredients, but it is more than just a pretty picture or—even less helpful—a montage that is not to scale so that a crab claw appears to be the same size as a duck. Instead, it serves as a handy way of checking that you have everything ready before you start cooking. Just comparing the picture with the ingredients arranged on your own counter or kitchen table will ensure that you haven't left anything out, and when it's time to add the cilantro, for example, you have already chopped it as specified in the ingredients list. If you're uncertain about how thinly to slice lemon grass or how finely to dice shrimp, a glance at the photograph will provide an instant answer.

Each short and straightforward step of the method is clearly explained without any jargon or difficult technical terms. Once again, what you see in the photograph is what you should expect to see in front of you. Not only is this reassuring for the novice cook, but those with more experience will also find it a helpful reminder of the little touches that can easily be overlooked. Each recipe ends with a mouthwatering photograph of the finished dish, complete with any serving suggestions.

Why you need this book

Asian food, whether Chinese, Thai, Japanese, Indonesian, or Malaysian, has been popular in the West for decades, and Western cooks have become increasingly adventurous about trying out recipes in their own kitchens, particularly since speciality ingredients have now become more widely available. Asian food is designed as much to please the eye as it is to please the palate and while many dishes, especially stir-fries, can be cooked in minutes, they are all prepared with attention to detail and an impressive balance of complementary flavors. The 60 easy-to-follow recipes in this book will enable you to re-create the authentic taste, texture, and appearance of Asia without leaving home.

You can simply pick and mix individual dishes for a midweek family supper or create a formal "banquet" for a special occasion with soup, wraps, stir-fries, curries, roasts, and, of course, rice and noodles, all arranged on the table together, followed by exotic ice cream or sticky fried fruit.

> 1 > 2 > 3

top tips for success

> Read all the way through the recipe—ingredients list and method—before you start so that you will know exactly what you will need. Scrabbling about at the back of the pantry to find a rarely used ingredient or moving half a dozen other utensils to reach the one you require in the middle of cooking a dish is, at best, exasperating and, at worst, liable to result in a scorched stir-fry or boiling-over rice.

> Do try to obtain the more unusual ingredients, such as galangal and Chinese chives—perhaps from a Chinese supermarket, which will often stock ingredients from many other Asian countries—to create a truly authentic flavor and unique aroma.

> Note that there is a difference between coconut milk, available in cans and extensively used in Thai and Indonesian cuisine, and the thin, almost colorless liquid found inside a fresh coconut. The canned milk is made by steeping shredded coconut flesh in water and is a thicker, creamy liquid.

> Always cut beef across the grain, otherwise it becomes tough. Lamb, pork, and poultry may be cut along or across the grain.

> If you need to cut meat into paper-thin slices, put it in the freezer for about 1 hour beforehand to firm up.

> A new wok should always be seasoned before it is used, unless it has a nonstick lining. This process seals the surface. First, scrub the wok with a cream cleanser to remove the manufacturer's protective coating of oil. Put the wok over a low heat and add 2 tablespoons vegetable oil. Make a pad of paper towels and wipe the oil all over the inside of the wok, then heat gently for about 10 minutes. Remove from the heat and wipe off the oil with more pads of paper towels, all of which will become black. Reheat the wok with another 2 tablespoons oil, spreading it over the surface with a pad of paper towels. Heat for another 10 minutes, then wipe out with pads of paper towels as before. Continue repeating this process until the pads of paper towels no longer turn black. The wok is now ready for use. (For additional information, see page 11.)

> There are two types of spring roll wrappers. Those made from rice flour must be soaked in water before using to make them flexible. Wheat flour wrappers are usually sold frozen. Let them thaw at room temperature for a couple of hours, then separate gently.

> Remember that Japanese soy sauce, sometimes simply called shoyu but also known as usukuchi (light) and tamari (regular), is not as strongly flavored as Chinese soy sauce.

time-saving shortcuts

> To peel garlic, lightly crush a clove with the flat blade of a cook's knife or cleaver. Then the skin is easy to remove.

> To prepare fresh ginger, peel off the skin with a paring knife. Put the ginger on a cutting board and lightly crush with the flat blade of a cook's knife or cleaver, then chop or cut into shreds.

> To prepare chiles, slice them lengthwise and scrape out the seeds and membranes with the tip of the knife. The heat of the chiles is in the membranes rather than the seeds, but removing the seeds tends to scrape out the membranes at the same time. If you like really fiery dishes, don't bother.

> To prepare lemon grass, cut off the dry tops to leave about 6 inches/15 cm stalk. Peel off any coarse outer layers. Put the lemon grass on a cutting board, put the flat side of a cook's knife or a cleaver on top, and hit it with your fist to bruise, then cut into thin slices. Finally, chop finely. You can also use lemon grass without chopping but, if you do, it must be removed and discarded before the dish is served.

> Use kitchen scissors to snip fresh herbs rather than chopping with a knife.

useful equipment

> **Wok:** This is probably the only essential piece of special equipment that isn't standard in a Western kitchen. It is a large, bowl-shaped pan—ideally about 14 inches/35 cm in diameter—with deep sloping sides and a round or flat bottom. Use the former with a metal stand on a gas burner and the latter on an electric one. It is primarily used for stir-frying, but is also useful for steaming, deep-frying, and braising. The best woks are made of carbon steel, which can withstand the high temperature required for stir-frying; stainless steel woks tend to scorch and nonstick woks must be used at lower than ideal temperatures. A wok with handles on either side is easy to lift. Others may have a single long handle or one long handle and one smaller,

ear-shaped handle opposite. A new wok must be seasoned before use (see page 10). If the wok is not supplied with a lid, it is worth buying a large, domed cover for steaming. It is possible to stir-fry in a large frying pan, but it is more difficult. The shape of the wok makes it very easy to toss the ingredients from the center to the sides without throwing them all over the stove. To stir-fry in a wok, preheat it thoroughly before adding any oil, which should then be swirled so that it covers the bottom and comes halfway up the sides. Start cooking with aromatics, then the ingredients that need the longest cooking time, and, finally, gradually add the rest.

> **Steamer:** A Western-style steamer may be used to cook Asian dishes, but it is worth considering buying bamboo steamers. They are inexpensive, designed to stack, and rest on the sloping sides of a wok just above the water level. They are available in a range of sizes and may also be used for serving. If you are planning to steam an ingredient, such as fish fillets, on a plate, you will require a trivet that can stand on the bottom of the wok and keep the plate above the water level.

> **Knives:** Good-quality, heavy, and well-balanced knives are essential in any kitchen. The minimum requirements are a paring, vegetable, utility, and chef's knife. Keep them sharpened using a V-sharpener, carborundum stone, or steel, and store them in a knife block. Sharp knives are not only easier to use, but are also safer because they are less liable to slip. Consider buying a cleaver. Most Western cooks find these heavy cutting tools somewhat unwieldy to begin with, but it is worth persevering because they serve many purposes from general chopping—including slicing effortlessly through ribs—to delicate tasks, such as deveining shrimp.

> **Cutting boards:** Wooden boards are inexpensive, have natural antibacterial properties, are gentle with knife blades, and are easy to wash or scrub in hot soapy water. Their disadvantages are that they are often heavy and bulky, so may cause storage problems, and they cannot be sterilized. Plastic boards have a rough texture to prevent slipping, are thinner and lighter, and can be washed in the dishwasher and sterilized. They usually come in a range of colors so it is easy to make sure that you use different boards for raw meat, poultry, and vegetables.

> **Wok accessories:** None of these is essential because you can use utensils easily found in any kitchen. However, they add to the authenticity and you may find them helpful. A wok scoop consists of a wide metal mesh basket on the end of a long wooden handle. It makes stir-frying easy, but you could use a long-handle spoon. A wok brush consists of a bundle of split bamboo used for cleaning your wok. You can simply use a dish-washing brush.

> **Cook's chopsticks:** These extra-long chopsticks can be used for adding ingredients, stirring, separating noodles, and fluffing up rice. Of course, you can use a spoon and a fork, but you'll have more fun using authentic implements, and they are much easier to manipulate than they seem at first sight. To use chopsticks, place one in the curve between your index finger and thumb. Pick up the second stick like a pencil. Keep the first stick still for stability and manipulate the second stick to pick up pieces of meat and vegetables.

appetizers
& soups

>4   >5   >6

thai tom yum soup with fish

serves 6

ingredients

6 cups light chicken stock
6 lemon grass stalks, crushed to
  release their flavor
3 tbsp very finely chopped
  cilantro roots
10 kaffir lime leaves, middle
  stalks torn off

1 red chile, seeded and finely
  chopped
1-inch/2.5-cm piece of
  galangal (or fresh ginger),
  peeled and thinly sliced
3 tbsp Thai fish sauce, plus extra
  to taste
1 tbsp sugar, plus extra to taste

1 lb 2 oz/500 g shrimp, peeled
  and deveined
1 lb 2 oz/500 g firm white fish,
  such as cod or monkfish,
  chopped into bite-size pieces
8 oz/225 g canned bamboo
  shoots or water chestnuts
12 cherry tomatoes, halved

juice of 2 limes
handful fresh cilantro leaves
  and handful fresh basil leaves,
  chopped, to garnish

> **1** Pour the stock into a large saucepan.

> **2** Add the lemon grass, cilantro roots, kaffir lime leaves, chile, galangal, Thai fish sauce, and sugar. Cover the saucepan.

> **3** Bring to a boil, then reduce the heat and simmer for 10 minutes.

> **4** Add the shrimp, fish, and bamboo shoots, and simmer for an additional 4 minutes.

17

>5 Add the tomatoes and lime juice and check the seasoning, adding more fish sauce and sugar, if necessary.

>6 Remove and discard the lemon grass stalks, then divide the soup among six bowls.

Scatter over the cilantro and
basil leaves and serve.

hot & sour soup tom yum

serves 4

ingredients

2 fresh red chiles, seeded
  and coarsely chopped
6 tbsp rice vinegar
5 cups vegetable stock
2 lemon grass stalks, halved

4 tbsp soy sauce
1 tbsp jaggery
juice of ½ lime
2 tbsp peanut or
  vegetable oil

8 oz/225 g firm tofu,
  drained and cut into
  ½-inch/1-cm cubes
14 oz/400 g canned straw
  mushrooms, drained

4 scallions, chopped
1 small head bok choy,
  shredded

>1 Mix the chiles and vinegar together in a nonreactive bowl, cover, and let stand at room temperature for 1 hour.

>2 Meanwhile, bring the stock to a boil in a saucepan. Add the lemon grass, soy sauce, jaggery, and lime juice, reduce the heat, and simmer for 20–30 minutes.

>3 Heat the oil in a preheated wok, add the tofu cubes, and stir-fry over a high heat for 2–3 minutes, or until browned all over. (You may need to do this in 2 batches, depending on the size of the wok.)

>4 Remove with a slotted spoon and drain on paper towels.

>5 Add the chiles and vinegar with the tofu, mushrooms, and half the scallions to the stock mixture and cook for 10 minutes.

>6 Mix the remaining scallions with the bok choy.

Scatter over the scallions and bok choy
and serve.

miso soup

serves 4

ingredients
4 cups water
2 tsp dashi granules
6 oz/175 g silken tofu, drained
  and cut into small cubes
4 shiitake mushrooms or white
  mushrooms, finely sliced
4 tbsp miso paste
2 scallions, chopped

>1 Put the water in a large pan with the dashi granules and bring to a boil.

>2 Add the tofu and mushrooms, reduce the heat, and let simmer for 3 minutes.

The miso paste will begin to settle, so stir the soup before serving to recombine.

> **3** Stir in the miso paste and let simmer gently, stirring, until it has dissolved.

> **4** Add the scallions and serve immediately.

thai salmon laksa

serves 4

ingredients

juice and zest of 2 limes
2 tbsp sunflower oil
1 red chile, seeded and finely
  chopped
4 garlic cloves, peeled and
  crushed

1-inch/2.5-cm piece fresh
  ginger, peeled and grated
1 tsp ground coriander
small bunch of fresh cilantro,
  plus extra to garnish
3 tbsp nam pla
2 cups vegetable or fish stock

3½ cups canned coconut milk
3 carrots, peeled and thinly
  sliced
14 oz/400 g noodles
1 tbsp sesame oil
1 tbsp vegetable oil
2¾ cups broccoli florets

1 lb 2 oz/500 g salmon fillet,
  skinned, boned, and cut into
  slices half the width of a finger

Put the first 8 ingredients in a food processor and blend to a paste.

Place a large saucepan over a medium heat and add the paste. Fry for 1 minute.

Add the stock, coconut milk, and carrots and bring to a boil. Simmer while you cook the noodles according to the package directions.

Drain the noodles and return to the warm saucepan with a splash of sesame oil and vegetable oil. Cover.

Add the broccoli to the liquid, bring back to a boil, and then turn off the heat and add the salmon slices, gently stirring them in. Let stand for 3 minutes.

> **6** Place a handful of noodles in each bowl, then ladle in the laksa.

Sprinkle with cilantro leaves
and serve.

chicken noodle soup

serves 4–6

ingredients

2 skinless chicken breasts

8 cups water

1 onion, with skin left on, cut in half

1 large garlic clove, cut in half

½-inch/1-cm piece fresh ginger, peeled and sliced

4 black peppercorns, lightly crushed

4 cloves

2 star anise

1 celery stalk, chopped

3½ oz/100 g baby corn cobs, sliced

2 scallions, finely shredded

4 oz/115 g dried rice vermicelli noodles

1 carrot, peeled and coarsely grated

salt and pepper

>**1** Put the chicken breasts and water in a saucepan and bring to a boil. Reduce the heat and simmer, skimming the surface until no more foam rises.

>**2** Add the onion, garlic, ginger, peppercorns, cloves, star anise, and a pinch of salt.

>**3** Continue to simmer for 20 minutes, or until the chicken is tender and cooked through.

>**4** Remove the chicken and set aside about 5 cups of stock. Add the celery, baby corn cobs, and scallions.

> **5** Bring the stock to a boil and boil until the baby corn cobs are almost tender, then add the noodles and continue boiling for 2 minutes.

> **6** Meanwhile, chop the chicken, add to the pan with the grated carrot, and continue cooking for about 1 minute, until the chicken is reheated and the noodles are soft. Add seasoning to taste.

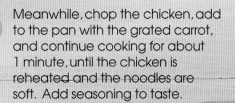

Transfer to bowls and serve.

hoisin & sesame-glazed broiled duck

serves 4

ingredients
2 duck breasts,
  about 8 oz/225 g each
½ tsp ground star anise
3 tbsp hoisin sauce
1 tbsp sesame oil
1 ripe mango
½ cucumber
4 scallions
1 tbsp rice vinegar
toasted sesame seeds,
  to sprinkle

>1 Using a sharp knife, score the skin of the duck breast in a diamond pattern.

>2 Mix the star anise, hoisin sauce, and sesame oil and brush over the duck. Cover and marinate for at least 30 minutes.

Serve the duck slices arranged over a spoonful of the mango salad, sprinkled with sesame seeds.

>3 Preheat the broiler to hot. Peel, pit, and thinly slice the mango. Cut the cucumber into matchsticks and thinly slice the onions. Stir together and sprinkle with the vinegar.

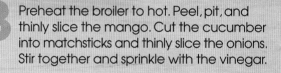

>4 Broil the duck for 8–10 minutes on each side, brushing with the marinade. Rest for 5 minutes, then slice thinly.

tempura vegetables

serves 4

ingredients
5½ oz/150 g package
   tempura mix
4 shiitake mushrooms
4 fresh asparagus spears
4 slices sweet potato

1 red bell pepper, seeded and
   cut into strips
4 onion slices, cut widthwise
   into rings
oil, for deep-frying

dipping sauce
2 tsp mirin
1 tbsp shoyu
   (Japanese soy sauce)

pinch of dashi granules,
   dissolved in 2 tbsp
   boiling water

> 1 To make the dipping sauce, mix the ingredients together in a small dipping dish.

> 2 Mix the tempura with water according to the package directions.

> 3 Drop the vegetables into the batter.

> 4 Heat enough oil for deep-frying in a wok, deep-fat fryer, or large heavy-bottom saucepan until it reaches 350–375°F/ 180–190°C, or until a cube of bread browns in 30 seconds.

Lift 2–3 pieces of the vegetables out of the batter, add to the oil, and cook for 2–3 minutes, or until the batter is a light golden color.

Remove the tempura vegetables with a slotted spoon and drain on paper towels. Keep hot while you cook the remaining pieces.

Transfer the tempura vegetables to a serving dish and serve with the dipping sauce.

pork & cabbage gyoza

makes 24

ingredients
24 gyoza wonton wrappers
2 tbsp water, for brushing
oil, for pan-frying
2 tbsp Japanese rice vinegar
2 tbsp shoyu (Japanese
  soy sauce)

filling
1½ cups finely shredded napa
  cabbage
2 scallions, finely chopped
4 oz/115 g fresh ground pork
½-inch/1-cm piece fresh ginger,
  finely grated

2 garlic cloves, crushed
1 tbsp shoyu (Japanese
  soy sauce)
2 tsp mirin
pinch of white pepper
salt, to taste

>1 To make the filling, mix all the ingredients together in a bowl.

>2 Lay a gyoza wonton wrapper in the palm of your hand and place 1 heaped teaspoon of the filling in the center. Brush a little water around the edges of the wonton wrapper.

>3 Fold the wrapper sides up to meet in a ridge along the center and press the edges together. Brush the curved edges of the wrapper with a little more water and make a series of little folds along the edges.

>4 Repeat with the remaining gyoza wonton wrappers and filling. Heat a little oil in a lidded deep skillet and add as many gyoza as will fill the bottom of the skillet with just a little space in between.

>5 Cook for 2 minutes, or until browned. Add water to a depth of 1/8 inch/3 mm, cover the skillet, and let simmer over a low heat for 6 minutes, or until the wrappers are translucent and cooked. Remove and keep warm while you cook the remaining gyoza.

>6 Put the vinegar in a small dipping dish, stir in the shoyu, and add a splash of water.

Transfer the gyoza to a serving
dish and serve with the sauce
for dipping.

shrimp toasts

makes 16 pieces

ingredients

3½ oz/100 g shrimp, peeled
  and deveined
2 egg whites
2 tbsp cornstarch
½ tsp sugar
pinch of salt
2 tbsp finely chopped fresh
  cilantro leaves
2 slices day-old white bread
vegetable or peanut oil, for
  deep-frying

> 1 Pound the shrimp to a pulp with a mortar and pestle.

> 2 Mix the shrimp with one of the egg whites and 1 tablespoon of the cornstarch. Add the sugar and salt and stir in the cilantro. Mix the remaining egg white with the remaining cornstarch.

Remove the prawn toasts with a slotted spoon, drain on kitchen paper and serve warm.

3 Remove the crusts from the bread and cut each slice into 8 triangles. Brush the top of each piece with the egg white-and-cornstarch mixture, then add 1 teaspoon of the shrimp mixture. Smooth the top.

4 Heat enough oil for deep-frying in a wok, deep-fat fryer, or large heavy-bottom saucepan until it reaches 350-375°F/180-190°C, or until a cube of bread browns in 30 seconds. Fry the toasts shrimp-side down for 2 minutes. Turn and fry for an additional 2 minutes, until golden.

45

chicken satay skewers with peanut sauce

serves 4

ingredients

4 skinless, boneless chicken
   breasts, about 4 oz/115 g
   each, cut into ¾-inch/2-cm
   cubes
4 tbsp soy sauce
1 tbsp cornstarch
2 garlic cloves, finely chopped

1-inch/2.5-cm piece fresh
   ginger, peeled and finely
   chopped
cucumber, coarsely chopped,
   to serve

peanut sauce

2 tbsp peanut or
   vegetable oil
½ onion, finely chopped
1 garlic clove, finely chopped
4 tbsp crunchy peanut butter
4–5 tbsp water
½ tsp chili powder

Put the chicken cubes in a shallow dish.

>2 Mix the soy sauce, cornstarch, garlic, and ginger together in a small bowl and pour over the chicken. Cover and let marinate in the refrigerator for at least 2 hours.

3 Meanwhile, soak 12 bamboo skewers in cold water for at least 30 minutes.

>4 Preheat the broiler. Thread the chicken pieces onto the bamboo skewers.

>5 Transfer the skewers to a broiler pan and cook under the preheated broiler for 3–4 minutes.

>6 Turn the skewers over and cook for an additional 3–4 minutes, or until cooked through.

>7 Meanwhile, to make the sauce, heat the oil in a saucepan, add the onion and garlic, and cook over a medium heat, stirring frequently, for 3–4 minutes until softened.

>8 Add the peanut butter, water, and chili powder and simmer for 2–3 minutes, until softened and thinned.

Serve the skewers immediately with the warm sauce and cucumber.

crab wontons

serves 4

ingredients

1 tbsp peanut or vegetable oil, plus extra for deep-frying
1-inch/2.5-cm piece fresh ginger, peeled and finely chopped

¼ red bell pepper, seeded and finely chopped
handful of fresh cilantro, chopped
¼ tsp salt

5½ oz/150 g canned white crabmeat, drained
20 wonton wrappers
water, for brushing
sweet chili dipping sauce, to serve

1 Heat the oil in a preheated wok.

 2 Add the ginger and red bell pepper and stir-fry over a high heat for 30 seconds.

3 Add the cilantro and mix well. Let cool, then add the salt and the crabmeat and mix well. Meanwhile, remove the wrappers from the package, but keep them in a pile covered with plastic wrap to prevent them from drying out.

4 Lay one wrapper on a work surface in front of you and brush the edges with water. Put a teaspoonful of the crabmeat mixture in the center and fold the wrapper over the mixture to form a triangle.

> **5** Press the edges together to seal. Fold each side corner up to the top corner to make a small parcel, brushing the edges with water to seal if necessary. Repeat with the remaining wrappers and crabmeat mixture.

> **6** Heat the oil for deep-frying in a wok, deep-fat fryer, or large heavy-bottom saucepan until it reaches 350-375°F/180–190°C, or until a cube of bread browns in 30 seconds.

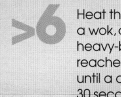

> **7** Add the wontons, in batches, and cook for 45 seconds–1 minute, until crisp and golden all over.

> **8** Remove with a slotted spoon, drain on pape towels, and keep warm while you cook the remaining wontons.

Serve with sweet chili dipping sauce.

vietnamese-style vegetable wraps

serves 4

ingredients

2 carrots
2 celery stalks
1 tbsp rice vinegar
½ tsp salt
2 scallions
2 cups bean sprouts
small handful cilantro leaves, chopped
small handful mint leaves, chopped
small handful basil leaves, chopped
8 Boston lettuce leaves

dressing

2 garlic cloves, chopped
1 red chile, seeded and chopped
1 tbsp jaggery
2 tbsp lime juice
2 tbsp Thai fish sauce

> **1** Slice the carrots and celery into fine matchsticks. Sprinkle with the vinegar and salt and let stand for 30 minutes. Drain.

> **2** Thinly slice the scallions and mix with the carrots, celery, bean sprouts, and herbs.

Transfer the wraps to a serving dish and serve with the remaining dressing.

>3 To make the dressing, mash the garlic, chile, and jaggery in a mortar and pestle, then stir in the lime juice, Thai fish sauce, and 2 tbsp water.

>4 Divide the vegetables between the lettuce leaves and spoon 1 teaspoon of the dressing over each leaf.

spring rolls

makes 20–25 pieces

ingredients

6 dried Chinese mushrooms,
  soaked in warm water for
  20 minutes
1 tbsp vegetable or peanut oil,
  plus extra for deep-frying
8 oz/225 g ground pork

1 tsp dark soy sauce
3½ oz/100 g canned bamboo
  shoots, rinsed and julienned
pinch of salt
3½ oz/100 g shrimp, peeled,
  deveined, and chopped

4 cups trimmed and coarsely
  chopped bean sprouts,
1 tbsp finely chopped scallions
20–25 spring roll wrappers
1 egg white, lightly beaten

1 Squeeze out any excess water from the mushrooms and finely slice, discarding any tough stems.

>2 Heat a wok or deep pan over high heat. Add 1 tbsp oil and heat until hot. Add the pork and stir-fry until it changes color.

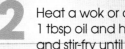

3 Add the dark soy sauce, bamboo shoots, mushrooms, and a little salt. Stir over a high heat for 3 minutes.

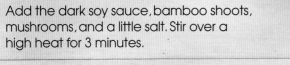

>4 Add the shrimp and cook for 2 minutes, then add the bean sprouts and cook for an additional minute. Remove from the heat and stir in the scallions. Let cool.

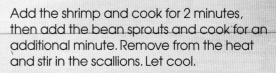

57

>5 Place a tablespoon of the mixture toward the bottom of a wrapper. Roll once to secure the filling, then fold in the sides to create a 4-inch/10-cm piece and continue to roll up. Seal with egg white.

>6 Heat enough oil for deep-frying in a wok, deep-fat fryer, or large heavy-bottom saucepan until it reaches 350–375°F/180–190°C, or until a cube of bread browns in 30 seconds. Fry the rolls for about 5 minutes, until golden brown and crispy.

Transfer the spring rolls to serving
bowls and serve.

sashimi

serves 2

ingredients

1 fresh (sushi-grade) mackerel,
  cleaned and filleted
⅓ cup rice vinegar
3 scallops, in their shells
5½ oz/150 g fresh (sushi-grade)
  tuna (maguro)
5½ oz/150 g fresh (sushi-grade)
  salmon (sake)

garnish

chopped daikon
fresh chives
sliced ginger
wasabi paste
shoyu (Japanese soy sauce),
  to serve

>1 Put the mackerel fillets and rice vinegar in a shallow, nonmetallic dish, cover with plastic wrap, and let marinate in the refrigerator for 1 hour.

>2 Remove the mackerel from the marinade and pat dry with paper towels. Skin, then slice the flesh diagonally.

>3 Remove the scallops from their shells. Separate any corals from the bodies, then remove and discard the white frills and any black matter and also the membrane around the edge of the scallops. Slice each scallop horizontally in half.

>4 Put the scallops in a heatproof dish and pour over boiling water to cover. Using a slotted spoon, remove immediately and pat dry with paper towels.

>5 Shape the tuna and salmon into neat rectangles, then slice into smaller rectangular slices.

>6 Arrange all the fish on a serving platter with the chopped daikon.

Garnish with fresh chives and serve with the
sliced ginger, wasabi paste, and shoyu.

sticky ginger & soy chicken wings

serves 4

ingredients
12 chicken wings
2 garlic cloves, crushed
1-inch/2.5-cm piece fresh
  ginger
2 tbsp dark soy sauce

2 tbsp lime juice
1 tbsp honey
1 tsp chili sauce
2 tsp sesame oil
lime wedges, to serve

>1 Tuck the pointed tip of each wing under the thicker end to make a neat triangle.

>2 Mix together the garlic, ginger, soy sauce, lime, honey, chili sauce, and oil.

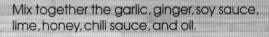

Serve hot with lime wedges.

3 Spoon the mixture over the chicken and turn to coat evenly. Cover and marinate for several hours or overnight.

>4 Preheat the broiler to hot. Cook the wings on a foil-lined broiler pan for 12–15 minutes, or until the juices have no trace of pink when pierced, basting often with the marinade.

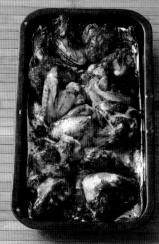

>1 >2 >3

noodles & rice

>4

>5

>6

scattered sushi & smoked mackerel

serves 4

ingredients

8 snow peas
2-inch/5-cm piece daikon
finely grated rind and juice of
  lemon
2 scallions, finely chopped

2 smoked mackerel, skinned
  and cut into diagonal strips
½ cucumber, peeled and cut
  into slices

garnish

pickled ginger
strips of toasted nori
wasabi paste

sushi rice

1 cup short-grain rice
1½ cups water
salt

1 Put the rice in a strainer and rinse in cold water until the water is clear, then drain.

>2 Put the rice in a pan with the water, cover, and bring to a boil as quickly as possible. Reduce the heat and simmer for 10 minutes. Turn off the heat and let stand for 15 minutes.

3 Transfer the rice to a bowl and add salt, to taste.

>4 Cook the snow peas in a pan of boiling salted water for 1 minute. Drain and cool.

>5 Using a sharp knife, shred the daikon into long, thin slices and cut each slice lengthwise as finely as you can.

>6 Mix the rice with the lemon rind and juice.

>7 Divide the cooked rice between 4 bowls and sprinkle the scallions over the top.

>8 Arrange the mackerel, cucumber, snow peas and daikon on top of the rice.

Garnish with pickled ginger, nori strips, and wasabi paste and serve.

udon noodle stir-fry with fish cakes & ginger

serves 2

ingredients

115 oz/300 g ready-to-wok
  udon noodles
1 leek, shredded
3½ cups bean sprouts
8 shiitake mushrooms, finely
  sliced

2 pieces Japanese fish cake,
  sliced
12 shrimp, peeled and
  deveined
2 eggs, beaten
oil, for stir-frying

2 tbsp shoyu (Japanese
  soy sauce)
3 tbsp mirin
2 tbsp chopped fresh
  cilantro leaves

to serve

chili oil
2 scallions, finely sliced
2 tbsp shredded beni-shoga
  (red ginger)

Rinse the noodles under cold running water to remove any oil and turn into a bowl.

Add the leek, bean sprouts, mushrooms, fish cake, shrimp, and eggs to the noodles and mix well to combine.

Heat a wok over high heat. Add a little oil and heat until very hot.

Add the noodle mixture and stir-fry until golden and the shrimp have turned pink and are cooked through.

>5 Add the shoyu, mirin, and cilantro and toss together.

>6 Divide the noodles between 2 bowls and drizzle with the chili oil.

Sprinkle with the scallions and
beni-shoga and serve.

yaki soba

serves 2

ingredients

14 oz/400 g ramen noodles
1 onion, finely sliced
3½ cups bean sprouts
1 red bell pepper, seeded
   and sliced
5½ oz/150 g chicken,
   cooked and sliced
12 cooked, peeled shrimp
1 tbsp oil, for stir-frying
2 tbsp shoyu
1 tsp sesame oil
1 tsp sesame seeds
2 scallions, finely sliced

> **1** Cook the noodles according to the package directions, drain well, and turn into a bowl.

> **2** Mix the onion, bean sprouts, red bell pepper, chicken, and shrimp together in a bowl. Stir through the noodles. Meanwhile, heat a wok over high heat, add the oil, and heat until very hot.

Sprinkle with sesame seeds and scallions and serve.

3 Add the noodle mixture and stir-fry for 4 minutes, or until golden, then add the shoyu, and sesame oil and toss together.

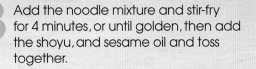

>4 Divide the noodles between two bowls.

crab, asparagus & shiitake rolls with ponzu sauce

makes 24 pieces

ingredients

6 fresh asparagus spears
1 tbsp oil
6 shiitake mushrooms, sliced
1 quantity of sushi rice
  (see page 68)

6 small sheets toasted nori
wasabi paste
6 crab sticks, split in half
  lengthwise

ponzu sauce
3 tbsp mirin
2 tbsp Japanese rice vinegar
1 tbsp usukuchi shoyu
  (Japanese light soy sauce)

2 tbsp bonito flakes
4 tbsp lemon juice

1 To make the sauce, put all the ingredients in a small pan and bring to a boil. Turn off the heat and let cool.

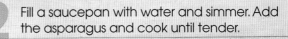

>2 Fill a saucepan with water and simmer. Add the asparagus and cook until tender.

3 Cut the asparagus spears into 3½-inch/9-cm pieces and let cool.

>4 Meanwhile, heat the oil in a skillet and cook the mushrooms over medium heat for 5 minutes, or until completely soft.

> **5** Divide the rice into 6 equal portions. Put a sheet of nori, shiny-side down, on a sushi rolling mat with the longest end toward you. Using wet hands, spread 1 portion of the rice in an even layer on the nori, leaving ¾ inch/2 cm of nori visible at the end furthest away from you.

> **6** Spread a small amount of wasabi onto the rice at the end nearest to you. Top with an asparagus spear, then add 2 pieces of crab stick alongside. Add a line of mushroom slice

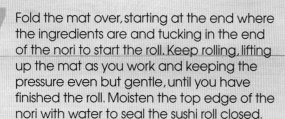

> **7** Fold the mat over, starting at the end where the ingredients are and tucking in the end of the nori to start the roll. Keep rolling, lifting up the mat as you work and keeping the pressure even but gentle, until you have finished the roll. Moisten the top edge of the nori with water to seal the sushi roll closed.

> **8** Remove the roll from the mat and cut into 4 even pieces with a wet, very sharp knife.

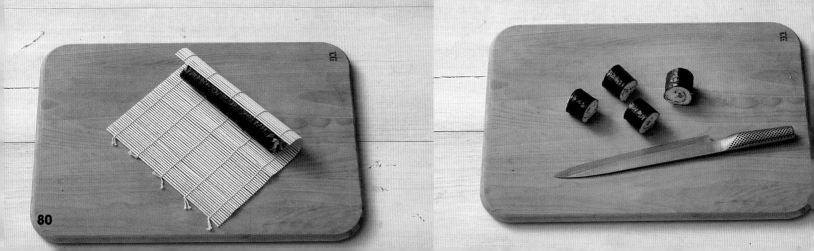

Repeat with the remaining ingredients
and serve with the ponzu sauce.

sesame noodles with shrimp

serves 2

ingredients

1 tbsp oil
16 shrimp, peeled and
  deveined
3 shiitake mushrooms, finely
  sliced

¼ white or green cabbage,
  shredded
1 carrot, grated
2 bundles of somen noodles
6 shiso leaves, shredded

dressing
3 tbsp oil
1 tbsp sesame seeds, toasted
½ cup Japanese rice vinegar
1 tbsp sugar

1 tbsp usukuchi shoyu
  (Japanese light soy sauce)
salt, to taste

>1 To make the dressing, mix the oil and all the remaining ingredients together in a nonmetallic bowl.

>2 Heat a wok, then add the oil and heat.

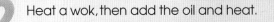

>3 Add the shrimp and cook until pink.

>4 Add the mushrooms and stir-fry for 1 minute, then add the cabbage and carrot. Remove from the heat and let cool.

>5 Cook the noodles according to the package directions, then drain.

>6 Put the noodles in a bowl, add the shrimp mixture and the dressing, and mix well.

Sprinkle with the shiso leaves and serve.

pho bo beef

serves 4

ingredients
8 cups rich beef stock
1 tbsp fresh ginger, finely sliced
1 garlic clove, thinly sliced
9 oz/250 g dried flat rice
  noodles
14 oz/400 g beef tenderloin or
  sirloin steak, thinly sliced into
  strips
4 scallions, thinly sliced
2¼ cups bean sprouts
2 tbsp Thai fish sauce
3 tbsp chopped fresh cilantro
chopped red chiles and soy
  sauce, to serve

> **>1** Heat the stock with the ginger and garlic until boiling, remove from the heat, and let infuse for 10 minutes.

> **>2** Cook the rice noodles in boiling water for 3–4 minutes, until just tender. Drain and divide between 4 deep bowls.

Serve the noodle soup immediately, with chiles and soy sauce to taste.

3 Top with the sliced beef and scallions, then strain over the boiling stock.

>4 Stir in the bean sprouts, fish sauce, and cilantro.

fragrant rice with lemon grass & ginger

serves 4

ingredients

1¼ cups jasmine rice
2 tbsp butter
1-inch/2.5-cm piece fresh
  ginger, grated

generous 1 cup canned
  coconut milk
generous 1 cup water
½ tsp salt
½ tsp superfine sugar

1 lemon grass stalk, bruised
2 dried kaffir lime leaves
curls of toasted fresh or dried
  coconut, to garnish

1 Soak the rice in cold water for 1 hour. Drain well.

>2 Melt the butter in a large pan and fry the rice on a high heat for 1 minute, stirring, until the grains are glossy.

3 Add the ginger and cook, stirring, for 30 seconds, or until browned.

>4 Stir in the coconut milk and water, then bring to a boil and add the salt and sugar.

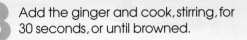

> **5** Reduce the heat and add the lemon grass and kaffir lime leaves. Cover and simmer gently for 10 minutes.

 Stir the rice, then place a dish towel over the pan, replace the lid, and let cook on a very low heat for 10 minutes.

Sprinkle with toasted coconut curls and serve as a side dish.

tea-smoked duck with jasmine rice

serves 4

ingredients

4 duck breasts, about 6 oz/
175 g each
2 tsp sea salt

1 tbsp Sichuan peppercorns,
without seeds, crushed
2 pieces star anise
⅓ cup black tea leaves

¼ cup rice
1 tbsp dark brown sugar
1⅔ cups jasmine rice

2 tbsp chopped cilantro leave
4 scallions, thinly sliced
diagonally

1 Score the skin of the duck breasts in a diamond pattern with a sharp knife.

>2 Mix the salt and crushed peppercorns and rub into the duck breasts. Cover and let stand for 1 hour.

3 Grind together the star anise, tea, rice, and sugar in a coffee grinder or processor. Line a wok with foil and scatter the mixture on the foil.

>4 Place a wire rack over the foil and arrange the duck breasts on top, skin-side down. Cover with a lid and tuck the foil around to seal.

>5 Place on a medium heat and when the tea begins to smoke, reduce the heat to low and cook for 10–12 minutes for rare, or 14–15 minutes for medium rare.

>6 Meanwhile, cook the jasmine rice in lightly salted boiling water for 10 minutes. Drain well and stir in the cilantro.

Slice the duck and serve with the jasmine rice, scattered with sliced scallions.

egg-fried rice
serves 4

ingredients
2 tbsp vegetable or peanut oil
2 cups cooked rice, chilled
1 egg, well beaten

>1 Heat a wok, then add the oil and heat. Add the rice and stir-fry for 1 minute.

>2 Using a fork, break down the rice as much as possible into individual grains.

Transfer the rice to bowls and serve.

Quickly add the egg, stirring to coat each piece of rice.

>4 Continue to stir until the egg is cooked and the rice, as far as possible, is in single grains.

97

pad noodles with pork strips & shrimp

serves 4

ingredients
9 oz/250 g flat rice noodles
7 oz/200 g pork tenderloin
3 tbsp peanut oil
2 shallots, finely chopped

2 garlic cloves, finely chopped
6 oz/175 g shrimp, peeled and
   deveined
2 eggs, beaten
2 tbsp Thai fish sauce

juice of 1 lime
1 tbsp ketchup
2 tsp light brown sugar
½ tsp dried chile flakes
1¾ cups bean sprouts

4 tbsp chopped, roasted salte
   peanuts
6 scallions, diagonally sliced

1 Soak the noodles in hot water for 10 minutes, or according to the package directions. Drain well.

>2 Slice the pork into strips about ¼ inch/ 5 mm thick.

3 Heat the oil in a wok and stir-fry the shallots for 1–2 minutes, until soft.

>4 Add the pork strips and stir-fry for 2–3 minutes.

>5 Add the garlic and shrimp and stir-fry for 1–2 minutes.

>6 Pour in the beaten eggs and stir for a few seconds until lightly set.

 >7 Reduce the heat and add the noodles, fish sauce, lime juice, ketchup, and sugar. Toss together and heat through.

>8 Sprinkle with chile flakes, bean sprouts, peanuts, and scallions.

Transfer to bowls and serve.

ho fun noodles with beef strips

serves 4

ingredients

10½ oz/300 g sirloin steak
2 tbsp soy sauce
2 tbsp sesame oil

9 oz/250 g flat rice noodles
2 tbsp peanut oil
1 onion, sliced into thin wedges
2 garlic cloves, crushed

1-inch/2.5-cm piece fresh
  ginger, chopped
1 red chile, thinly sliced
7 oz/200 g sprouting broccoli

½ Chinese cabbage, sliced
chili oil, to serve

1 Slice the beef into thin strips, place in a bowl, and sprinkle with soy sauce and sesame oil. Cover and let stand for 15 minutes.

>2 Soak the noodles in hot water for 10 minutes or according to the package directions. Drain well.

3 Heat 1 tablespoon of peanut oil in a wok over high heat and stir-fry the beef until evenly colored. Remove and keep to one side.

>4 Add the remaining oil and stir-fry the onion, garlic, ginger, and chile for 1 minute.

>5 Add the broccoli and stir-fry for 2 minutes, then add the cabbage and stir-fry for 1 minute.

>6 Add the beef with any marinade juices and stir until thoroughly heated, then spoon onto the noodles.

Serve immediately, drizzled with chili oil.

chicken fried rice

serves 4

ingredients

½ tbsp sesame oil

6 shallots, peeled and cut into quarters

3 cups cubed cooked chicken

3 tbsp soy sauce

2 carrots, diced

1 celery stalk, diced

1 red bell pepper, seeded and diced

1¼ cups fresh peas

⅔ cup drained canned corn kernels

1¾ cups cooked long-grain rice

2 large eggs

> **1** Heat a wok or large skillet over a medium heat, add the oil, and heat it.

> **2** Add the shallots and fry until soft, then add the chicken and 2 tablespoons of the soy sauce and stir-fry for 5–6 minutes.

Transfer to bowls and serve immediately.

3 Stir in the carrots, celery, red bell pepper, peas, and corn and stir-fry for an additional 5 minutes.

>4 Add the rice and stir thoroughly. Beat the eggs and pour into the mixture. Stir until the eggs are beginning to set, then add in the remaining soy sauce.

egg noodles with tofu & mushrooms

serves 4

ingredients

3 tbsp peanut oil

2 dried red chiles

9 oz/250 g medium egg noodles

1 garlic clove, crushed

7 oz/200 g firm tofu, cut into ½-inch/1-cm cubes

7 oz/200 g oyster or cremini mushrooms, sliced

2 tbsp lime juice

2 tbsp soy sauce

1 tsp brown sugar

fresh red chiles, to garnish

> 1 Heat the oil in a wok and add the chiles. Heat gently for 10 minutes. Discard the fried chiles.

> 2 Cook the noodles in boiling water for 4 minutes, or according to the package directions. Drain.

> 3 Add the garlic and tofu to the wok and stir-fry on a high heat until golden. Remove with a slotted spoon and keep hot.

> 4 Add the mushrooms to the wok and stir-fry for 2–3 minutes to soften.

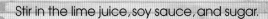

>5 Stir in the lime juice, soy sauce, and sugar.

>6 Return the noodles and tofu to the wok and toss to mix thoroughly.

Serve immediately, garnished with fresh chiles.

thai noodle salad

serves 4

ingredients

7 oz/200 g fine rice noodles
2 tbsp peanut oil
1 red onion, thinly sliced
2 carrots, cut into matchsticks

4½ oz/125 g baby corn, halved
  lengthwise
1 garlic clove, crushed
2¾ cups bean sprouts
2 tbsp Thai fish sauce

juice of ½ lime
1 tsp superfine sugar
½ tsp dried chile flakes
4 tbsp chopped cilantro
4 scallions, thinly sliced

¼ cup toasted peanuts
lime wedges, to serve

1 Soak the noodles in hot water for 10 minutes, or according to the package directions. Drain well.

>2 Heat the oil in a wok and stir-fry the onion for 1 minute.

3 Add the carrots and corn and stir-fry for 2 minutes. Stir in the garlic, then remove from the heat.

>4 Stir in the bean sprouts, then turn into a bowl and add the noodles, tossing to mix evenly.

Mix together the fish sauce, lime juice, superfine sugar, chile flakes, and half the cilantro.

Spoon into serving bowls, then sprinkle with scallions, peanuts, and the remaining cilantro.

Serve hot with lime wedges.

crispy noodles with bok choy in oyster sauce

serves 4

ingredients

peanut oil, for deep-frying
3½ oz/100 g dried rice
  vermicelli noodles
1 tbsp crushed jaggery or
  brown sugar
1 tbsp rice vinegar
1 tbsp Thai fish sauce
1 tbsp lime juice
6 scallions, sliced
1 garlic clove, thinly sliced
12 oz/350 g baby bok choy,
  quartered lengthwise
3 tbsp oyster sauce
sesame seeds, to sprinkle

>1 Heat a deep pan of oil until a piece of noodle sizzles instantly. Add the noodles and fry in batches for 15–20 seconds, until puffed and golden. Drain on paper towels.

>2 Heat the sugar, vinegar, fish sauce, and lime juice in a small pan, until the sugar dissolves. Boil for 20–30 seconds, until syrupy.

Serve the dish immediately,
sprinkled with sesame seeds.

>3 Heat 2 tablespoons of the oil in a wok
and stir-fry the scallions and garlic for
1 minute. Add the bok choy and stir-fry
for 2–3 minutes. Stir in the oyster sauce.

>4 Toss the noodles with the syrup and serve with
the bok choy.

>1

>2

>3

main
meals

>4

>5

>6

gado gado

serves 4

ingredients

2 shallots, finely chopped
2 garlic cloves, crushed
3 tbsp peanut oil
1 red chile, finely chopped

juice of 2 limes
1 cup crunchy peanut butter
generous 1 cup coconut
  milk
7 oz/200 g green beans

½ cucumber
1 red bell pepper
9 oz/250 g tempeh or firm tofu,
  diced
3½ cups bean sprouts

2 heads Boston lettuce,
  chopped
2 hard-boiled eggs, quartered
chopped cilantro, to garnish

1 Fry the shallots and garlic in 1 tablespoon of the oil for 2–3 minutes to soften but not brown.

>2 Stir in the chile, lime juice, peanut butter, and coconut milk, and stir over a medium heat for 2–3 minutes. Cool.

3 Cut the beans into bite-size pieces, then blanch in boiling water for 2 minutes. Drain and rinse in cold water.

>4 Halve the cucumber lengthwise and slice diagonally. Seed and thinly slice the red bell pepper.

>5 Heat the remaining oil in a skillet and fry the tempeh until golden on all sides. Drain on absorbent paper towels.

>6 Toss together the beans, cucumber, red bell pepper, bean sprouts, and lettuce and arrange on a large platter.

>7 Arrange the fried tempeh and hard-boiled eggs over the salad.

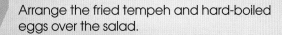

>8 Spoon the dressing onto the salad and sprinkle with chopped cilantro.

Serve immediately.

seafood curry

serves 4

ingredients

2 dried red chiles
2 tsp coriander seeds
1 tsp cumin seed
2 cardamom pods
1 tsp fenugreek seeds
1 tsp black peppercorns

1 tsp turmeric
1 tsp salt
1 lb 2 oz/500 g mixed fish fillets, such as tuna, or mackerel
3 tbsp peanut oil
1 large onion, chopped
2 garlic cloves, crushed

1-inch/2.5-cm piece fresh ginger, finely chopped
1¾ cups canned coconut milk
14 oz/400 g canned chopped plum tomatoes

6 oz/175 g shrimp, peeled and deveined
chopped fresh cilantro, to garnish

1 Place the chiles, coriander seeds, cumin, cardamom, fenugreek, and peppercorns in a heavy-bottom pan and stir on a high heat for 1 minute.

>2 Crush the spices finely with a mortar and pestle and add the turmeric and salt.

3 Cut the fish into 2-inch/5-cm chunks and rub with half the spices. Cover and set aside.

>4 Heat half the oil in a large pan and fry the onion gently for 10 minutes, until soft and golden.

>5 Add the garlic, ginger, and remaining spices and stir-fry for 1 minute.

>6 Mix ⅓ cup of water with the coconut milk. Add to the pan with the tomatoes, cover, and simmer for 15 minutes.

>7 Heat the remaining oil in a skillet and fry the fish quickly until lightly browned.

>8 Add the fish and shrimp to the sauce and simmer for 5–6 minutes.

Serve the curry immediately, garnished with chopped fresh cilantro.

green chicken curry

serves 4

ingredients

2 tbsp peanut or
  vegetable oil
4 scallions, roughly chopped
2 tbsp green curry paste
3 cups canned coconut milk
1 chicken stock cube
6 skinless, boneless chicken
  breasts, cut into 1-inch/2.5-cm
  cubes
large handful of fresh cilantro,
  chopped
1 tsp salt
cooked rice, to serve

> **1** Heat a wok over medium–high heat, add the oil, and heat. Add the scallions and stir-fry for 30 seconds, or until starting to soften.

> **2** Add the curry paste, coconut milk, and stock cube and bring gently to a boil, stirring occasionally.

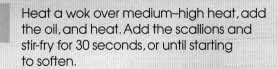

Serve immediately with rice.

3 Add the chicken cubes, half the cilantro, and the salt and stir well. Reduce the heat and simmer gently for 8–10 minutes, until the chicken is cooked through and tender.

>4 Stir in the remaining cilantro.

teriyaki chicken

serves 4

ingredients

4 skinless, boneless chicken
  breasts, about 6 oz/175 g
  each

4 tbsp teriyaki sauce
peanut or corn oil, for brushing

sesame noodles
9 oz/250 g dried thin
  buckwheat noodles
1 tbsp toasted sesame oil

2 tbsp sesame seeds, toasted
2 tbsp finely chopped fresh
  parsley
salt and pepper

1 Using a sharp knife, score each chicken breast diagonally across 3 times. Rub all over with teriyaki sauce. Set aside in the refrigerator to marinate for at least 10 minutes or up to 24 hours.

>2 Preheat the broiler to high. Bring a saucepan of water to a boil, add the buckwheat noodles, and cook according to the package directions. Drain and rinse well in cold water.

3 Lightly brush the broiler pan with oil. Add the chicken breasts and brush again with a little extra teriyaki sauce.

>4 Broil the chicken breast, brushing occasionally with extra teriyaki sauce, for 15 minutes, or until cooked through and the juices run clear when pierced with a skewer.

131

>5 Meanwhile, heat a wok over high heat. Add the sesame oil and heat until it shimmers.

>6 Add the noodles and stir around to heat through, then stir in the sesame seeds and parsley. Add salt and pepper to taste.

Transfer the chicken breasts to plates and add a portion of noodles to each.

chicken with cashew nuts

serves 4–6

ingredients

1 lb/450 g boneless, skinless
  chicken, cut into bite-size
  pieces
3 tbsp light soy sauce
1 tsp Shaoxing rice wine

pinch of sugar
½ tsp salt
3 dried Chinese mushrooms,
  soaked in warm water for
  20 minutes
2 tbsp vegetable or peanut oil

4 slices fresh ginger
1 tsp finely chopped garlic
1 red bell pepper, seeded and
  cut into 1-inch/2.5-cm squares
⅔ cup toasted cashew nuts

1 Marinate the chicken in 2 tablespoons of the light soy sauce, Shaoxing, sugar, and salt for at least 20 minutes.

>2 Squeeze any excess water from the mushrooms and finely slice, discarding any tough stems. Reserve the soaking water.

3 Heat a wok, add 1 tablespoon of the oil, and heat it. Add the ginger and stir-fry until fragrant. Stir in the chicken and cook for 2 minutes, until it turns brown. Before the chicken is cooked through, remove and set aside.

>4 Clean the wok, heat the remaining oil, and stir-fry the garlic until fragrant. Add the mushrooms and red bell pepper and stir-fry for 1 minute.

135

>5 Add about 2 tablespoons of the mushroom soaking water and cook for about 2 minutes, until the water has evaporated.

>6 Return the chicken to the wok, add the remaining light soy sauce and the cashew nuts, and stir-fry for 2 minutes, until the chicken is cooked through.

Transfer to bowls and serve.

peking duck

serves 6–10

ingredients
1 duck, weighing 4 lb 8 oz/2 kg
6 cups boiling water
1 tbsp honey
1 tbsp Shaoxing rice wine
1 tsp white rice vinegar
10 scallions
1 cucumber, peeled, seeded,
  and julienned
30 pancakes
plum or hoisin sauce, to serve

>1 To prepare the duck, massage the skin to separate it from the meat. Pour the boiling water into a large pan, add the honey, Shaoxing, and vinegar, and lower in the duck. Baste for about 1 minute. Remove the duck and hang it to dry for 2 hours, or overnight.

>2 Preheat the oven to 400°F/200°C. Place the duck on a rack above a roasting pan and roast for at least 1 hour, until the skin is crispy and the duck is cooked through.

Roll up and eat. Repeat the process
with the lean meat.

>3 Shred the white parts of the scallions.
Place the duck on a cutting board,
together with the cucumber, scallions,
and pancakes, and carve off the skin first.

>4 On a pancake, arrange a little skin with some
cucumber and scallion, then top with a little
plum sauce.

ginger pork with shiitake mushrooms

serves 4

ingredients

2 tbsp vegetable oil
3 shallots, finely chopped
2 garlic cloves, crushed
2-inch/5-cm piece fresh ginger, thinly sliced

1 lb 2 oz/500 g pork, cut into strips
9 oz/250 g shiitake mushrooms, sliced
4 tbsp soy sauce
4 tbsp rice wine

1 tsp light brown sugar
1 tsp cornstarch
2 tbsp cold water
3 tbsp chopped fresh cilantro, to garnish

1 Heat the oil in a wok and fry the shallots for 2–3 minutes to soften.

>2 Add the garlic and ginger and stir-fry for 1 minute.

3 Add the pork strips and stir-fry for 1 minute.

>4 Add the mushrooms and stir-fry for an additional 2–3 minutes.

>5 Stir in the soy sauce, rice wine, and sugar.

>6 Blend the cornstarch and water until smooth, add to the pan, stirring, and cook until the juices are thickened and clear.

Serve the stir-fry garnished with cilantro.

fried tofu with lemon grass

serves 6

ingredients

3 tbsp Thai fish sauce

3 tbsp freshly squeezed lime or lemon juice

3 tbsp jaggery or granulated sugar

1 lemon grass stalk

vegetable oil, for frying

1 large shallot, finely chopped

1 large garlic clove, finely chopped

1 Thai chile, seeded and finely chopped

2 lb/900 g firm or extra-firm tofu, drained and cut crosswise into ½ inch/1 cm thick rectangular slices

6 sprigs fresh cilantro, trimmed to garnish

1 Put the Thai fish sauce, lime juice, and sugar in a nonmetallic bowl and whisk until the sugar is completely dissolved. Reserve.

>2 Discard the bruised leaves and root end of the lemon grass stalk, then finely grate 6–8 inches/15–20 cm of the lower stalk.

3 Heat 2 tablespoons of oil in a small saucepan over a high heat, then add the lemon grass, shallot, garlic, and chile and stir-fry for 5 minutes, or until fragrant and golden.

>4 Transfer to the fish sauce mixture and stir well. Reserve.

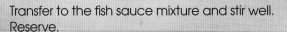

>5 Working in batches if necessary, heat 2 tablespoons of oil in a nonstick skillet, then add the tofu slices and fry over a high heat, turning often, for 6 minutes, or until golden and crisp on both sides.

>6 Drain on a plate lined with paper towels. If cooking in batches, add extra oil to the skillet as needed. Transfer to plates and serve.

Transfer the fried tofu to a serving platter and spoon the herb sauce over each slice, then garnish with the cilantro sprigs.

beef chop suey

serves 4

ingredients
1 lb/450 g rib-eye steak, sliced
1 head broccoli, cut into florets
2 tbsp vegetable oil
1 onion, sliced
2 celery stalks, sliced
8 oz/225 g snow peas, sliced lengthwise
¾ cup canned bamboo shoots, shredded
8 water chestnuts, sliced
8 oz/225 g mushrooms, sliced
1 tbsp oyster sauce
1 tsp salt

marinade
1 tbsp Shaoxing rice wine
½ tsp white pepper
½ tsp salt
1 tbsp light soy sauce
½ tsp sesame oil

> 1 Combine all the marinade ingredients in a bowl, and marinate the beef for at least 20 minutes.

>2 Blanch the broccoli in a large pan of boiling water for 30 seconds. Drain and set aside.

Transfer to bowls and serve.

3 Heat a wok, add 1 tablespoon of the oil, and heat. Add the beef and stir-fry until the color has changed. Remove and set aside.

4 Clean the wok, heat the remaining oil, and stir-fry the onion for 1 minute. Add the celery and broccoli and cook for 2 minutes. Add the snow peas, bamboo shoots, water chestnuts, and mushrooms and cook for 1 minute. Add the beef and season with the oyster sauce and salt.

sichuan noodles

serves 4

ingredients

9 oz/250 g thick egg noodles
2 tbsp peanut or corn oil
2 large garlic cloves, finely
chopped

1 large red onion, cut in half
and thinly sliced
½ cup vegetable stock or
water
2 tbsp chili bean sauce

2 tbsp Chinese sesame paste
1 tbsp dried Sichuan
peppercorns, roasted and
ground
1 tsp light soy sauce

2 baby bok choys or other
Chinese cabbage, cut into
quarters
1 large carrot, grated

>1 Cook the noodles in a saucepan of boiling water for 4 minutes, or according to package directions, until soft.

>2 Drain and rinse with cold water and set aside.

>3 Heat a wok over high heat and add the oil.

>4 Add the garlic and onion and stir-fry for 1 minute.

151

> **5** Add the vegetable stock, chili bean sauce, sesame paste, ground Sichuan peppercorns, and soy sauce and bring to a boil, stirring to blend the ingredients together.

> **6** Add the bok choy quarters and grated carro and continue to stir-fry for 1–2 minutes, until they are just wilted.

> **7** Add the noodles and continue stir-frying,

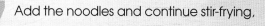

> **8** Using 2 forks, mix all the ingredients together until the noodles are hot.

Transfer to bowls and serve.

red-cooked duck with bamboo shoots

serves 4

ingredients

5 lb 8 oz/2.5 kg oven-ready
  duck with giblets
3 shallots, chopped
2 garlic cloves, sliced

1-inch/2.5-cm piece fresh
  ginger, sliced
2 tsp Chinese five spice paste
2 pieces star anise
scant ½ cup rice wine

3 tbsp soy sauce
2 tbsp brown sugar
4 cups water, approx.
1 tsp cornstarch
4 tbsp plum sauce

8 oz/225 g canned bamboo
  shoots, drained and cut into
  matchsticks
chopped cilantro, to garnish
boiled rice, to serve

1 Place the duck in a large pan, breast-side down. Add the shallots, garlic, ginger, spice paste, anise, rice wine, soy sauce, and sugar.

2 Pour over just enough water to cover the duck. Bring to a boil, cover, and simmer for 1 hour, turning once.

3 Lift out the duck and discard the giblets. Cut the duck into 8 pieces, discarding the backbone.

>4 Strain the liquid, skim off the fat, and boil to reduce to about 2 cups.

>**5** Mix the cornstarch with 1 tbsp cold water, stir into the sauce, and cook until thickened. Add the plum sauce.

>**6** Add the duck pieces to the sauce and simmer for 8–10 minutes, turning occasionally. Add the bamboo shoots.

Serve the duck with boiled rice, sprinkled
with cilantro.

sliced beef in black bean sauce

serves 4

ingredients

3 tbsp peanut oil
1 lb/450 g porterhouse steak,
  thinly sliced
1 red bell pepper, seeded and
  thinly sliced
1 green bell pepper, seeded
  and thinly sliced
1 bunch scallions, sliced
2 garlic cloves, crushed
1 tbsp grated fresh ginger
2 tbsp black bean sauce
1 tbsp sherry
1 tbsp soy sauce

> **>1** Heat 2 tbsp oil in a wok over high heat and stir-fry the beef for 1–2 minutes. Remove the beef and set aside.

> **>2** Add the remaining oil and peppers to the wok and stir-fry for 2 minutes.

Transfer to bowls and serve.

3 Add the scallions, garlic, and ginger and stir-fry for 30 seconds.

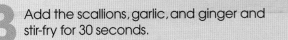

>4 Add the black bean sauce, sherry, and soy sauce, then stir in the beef and heat until bubbling.

honey-glazed roast pork

serves 4

ingredients

2 tbsp honey
1 tbsp rice vinegar
2 tbsp light brown sugar
1 tbsp hoisin sauce

1 tbsp light soy sauce
2 tsp five spice paste
1 lb 2 oz/500 g pork tenderloin,
  in one piece
3 tbsp rice wine

1 tsp cornstarch
¾ cup chicken stock
stir-fried vegetables, to serve

1 Mix together the honey, vinegar, sugar, hoisin sauce, and soy sauce in a wide, nonmetallic bowl with the spice paste. Pour over the pork. Cover and let marinate in the refrigerator overnight.

>2 Preheat the oven to 400°F/200°C. Drain the pork, reserving the marinade, and place on a wire rack in a roasting pan.

3 Pour boiling water into the pan until 1-inch/2.5-cm deep and place in the oven for 20 minutes.

>4 Turn the pork over, brush with the marinade, then cook for an additional 20 minutes, or until there is no trace of pink in the juices.

Mix the rice wine and cornstarch to a
smooth paste, then place in a pan with the
reserved marinade and stock.

Bring to a boil while stirring, then
simmer for 2 minutes, until thickened
and clear.

Slice the pork thinly and serve with the sauce spooned over. Serve with stir-fried vegetables.

thai fish cakes

serves 4

ingredients

1 garlic clove, sliced
1 shallot, finely chopped
1 lemon grass stalk, finely chopped
1-inch/2.5-cm piece galangal, finely chopped

4 tbsp cilantro, chopped
1 tbsp Thai fish sauce
1 small egg, beaten
1 lb 2 oz/500 g skinless white fish fillets
peanut oil, for frying

sauce

2-inch/5-cm piece cucumber
1 small red chile
1 tsp jaggery or dark brown sugar
juice of 1 lime
2 tbsp light soy sauce

1 Place the garlic, shallot, lemon grass, galangal, cilantro, Thai fish sauce, and egg in a food processor and process until smooth.

>2 Cut the fish into chunks, add to the processor, and process in short bursts until very finely chopped.

3 Divide the mixture into 12–16 pieces, roll into balls with your hands, then flatten into patty shapes.

>4 To make the sauce, cut the cucumber into fine dice and finely chop the chile.

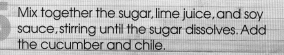

>5 Mix together the sugar, lime juice, and soy sauce, stirring until the sugar dissolves. Add the cucumber and chile.

>6 Heat a shallow depth of oil in a skillet and fry the fish cakes in batches until golden, turning once.

>7 Lift out the fish cakes and drain on absorbent paper towels.

>8 Cook the remaining fish cakes in the same way and tansfer to paper towels.

Serve the fish cakes hot, with the chili sauce for dipping.

sichuan peppered beef

serves 4

ingredients
1-inch/2.5-cm piece fresh
  ginger, grated
1 garlic clove, crushed
1 tbsp rice wine
1 tbsp soy sauce
1 tbsp hoisin sauce
2 tsp Sichuan peppercorns,
  without seeds, crushed
1 lb 5 oz/600 g beef tenderloin
3 tbsp peanut oil
1 onion, thinly sliced
1 green bell pepper, seeded
  and thinly sliced

> **>1** Mix together the ginger, garlic, rice wine, soy sauce, hoisin sauce, and peppercorns in a wide, nonmetallic bowl.

> **>2** Thinly slice the beef into medallions and add to the bowl, turning to coat in the marinade. Cover and let marinate for 30 minutes.

Serve the beef immediately.

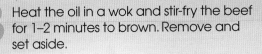

>3 Heat the oil in a wok and stir-fry the beef for 1–2 minutes to brown. Remove and set aside.

>4 Add the onion and green bell pepper and stir-fry for 2 minutes. Add the beef with any marinade juices and stir to heat evenly.

desserts

>4

>5

>6

coconut pancakes with pineapple

serves 4

ingredients

1¼ cups all-purpose flour
2 tbsp superfine sugar
2 eggs

1¾ cups canned coconut milk
1 medium pineapple
peanut oil, for frying
toasted coconut, to decorate

canned coconut cream,
  to serve (optional)

1 Sift the flour and sugar into a bowl and make a well in the center.

>2 Add the eggs and coconut milk to the well and stir into the flour, then whisk to a smooth, bubbly batter.

3 Cut off the skin of the pineapple, remove the core, and cut the flesh into chunks.

>4 Heat a small amount of oil in a heavy-bottom skillet over high heat and pour in a little batter, swirling to cover the pan.

Cook the pancake until set and
golden underneath.

Toss or turn the pancake and cook until
golden on the other side.

>7 Repeat with the remaining batter to make
8–10 pancakes, stacking alternately with wax
paper between while making the rest.

>8 Fill the pancakes with pieces of pineapple
and fold into fan shapes to serve.

Sprinkle the pancakes with toasted shreds of coconut and serve drizzled with coconut cream, if you like.

green tea ice cream

serves 4

ingredients

1 cup milk
2 egg yolks

2 tbsp superfine sugar
2 tbsp green tea powder
⅓ cup hot water

1 cup heavy cream, lightly
  whipped

1 Pour the milk into a pan and heat until it reaches boiling point. Meanwhile, whisk the egg yolks with the sugar in a heatproof bowl.

>2 Pour the milk onto the egg mixture, stirring constantly, then pour all the mixture back into the pan and stir well.

3 Cook over low heat, stirring constantly, for 3 minutes, or until the mixture is thick enough to coat the back of a spoon. Remove from the heat and let cool.

>4 Mix the green tea powder with the hot water in a pitcher or measuring cup, pour into the cooled custard, and mix well.

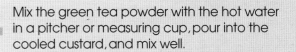

5 Fold in the cream. Transfer to a freezerproof container and freeze for 2 hours.

6 Turn into a bowl and beat with a fork to break down the ice crystals, then return to the freezerproof container and freeze for an additional 2 hours. Beat again, then return to the freezer and freeze overnight, or until solid.

Transfer to bowls and serve.

coconut ice cream

serves 4

ingredients
1¾ cups canned coconut milk
¾ cup superfine sugar
⅔ cup light cream
rind of ½ lime, finely grated
2 tbsp lime juice
curls of lime zest, to decorate

> **1** Place half the coconut milk and the sugar in a pan over medium heat and stir until the sugar dissolves.

> **2** Remove from the heat and stir in the remaining coconut milk, cream, and lime rind and juice. Let cool completely.

Top with curled shreds of lime
zest and serve.

>3 Transfer to a freezerproof container
and freeze for 2 hours, beating at
hourly intervals.

>4 Serve the ice cream scooped into glasses or
bowls.

almond-tea gelatins

serves 4–6

ingredients

14½ oz/410 g canned
  evaporated milk
¼ cup rice flour

¼ cup superfine sugar
½ cup ground almonds
1 tsp almond extract
1 envelope of gelatin

4 tbsp hot water
2 tsp jasmine blossom tea
  leaves
rose petals, to decorate

1
Place the evaporated milk and rice flour in a pan and heat, stirring, until boiling.

>2
Remove from the heat and stir in the sugar, almonds, and almond extract. Cover and let stand for 10 minutes.

3
Dissolve the gelatin in a bowl with the water placed over a pan of hot water.

>4
Stir the gelatin mixture into the milk mixture.

>5 Spoon the mixture into a 7-inch/18-cm square shallow cake pan. Chill to set.

 >6 Pour a generous 1 cup boiling water over th jasmine tea and let infuse for 4 minutes.

>7 Strain the tea, then let cool and chill in the refrigerator.

 >8 Cut the almond gelatin into diamond shape and arrange in wide individual bowls.

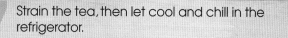

Spoon the tea around the diamond-shape gelatins and scatter with rose petals to serve.

spiced mung bean pots

serves 6

ingredients

generous ⅓ cup mung beans
½ cup superfine sugar

2 tbsp rice flour
½ tsp ground cinnamon
½ tsp ground ginger

finely grated rind 1 lime
1 large egg
½ cup canned coconut milk

whipped cream and freshly
grated nutmeg, to serve

> 1 Place the beans in a pan and cover with boiling water. Bring to a boil, cover, and simmer for about 30 minutes, or until tender.

> 2 Drain the beans well and press through a strainer to make a smooth puree.

> 3 Sift the sugar, flour, and spices into a bowl and add the bean puree and lime rind.

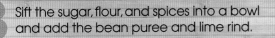

> 4 Beat the egg with the coconut milk and stir into the bowl, mixing evenly.

Place a steamer over high heat. Spoon the mixture into six ½-cup heatproof dishes.

>6 Cover the dishes tightly with foil and place in the steamer.

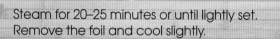

>7 Steam for 20–25 minutes or until lightly set. Remove the foil and cool slightly.

>8 To serve, top with a spoonful of whipped cream and sprinkle with nutmeg.

Serve immediately.

lychee sherbert

serves 4

ingredients

14 oz/400 g canned lychees,
 or 1 lb/450 g fresh lychees,
 peeled and pitted

2 tbsp confectioners' sugar
1 egg white
1 lemon, thinly sliced,
 to decorate

>1 Put the lychee flesh into a blender or food processor with the sugar. Blend to a puree.

>2 Press the lychee puree through a strainer to remove any remaining solid pieces.

Decorate with lemon slices and serve.

>3 Transfer to a freezerproof container and freeze for 3 hours.

>4 Turn the mixture into the blender or food processor and blend until slushy. Keeping the motor running, add the egg white, then return the mixture to the freezerproof container and freeze for 8 hours or overnight.

fried banana dumplings

serves 6

ingredients

vegetable oil, for deep-frying
1¼ cups all-purpose flour
2 tbsp granulated sugar or
  jaggery

½ tsp salt
2 tsp baking powder
2 large eggs
1½ cups canned coconut
  milk

12 small, ripe Asian bananas,
  peeled
confectioners' sugar, for dusting

Fill a small to medium saucepan halfway with oil and heat over a medium–high heat to 350–375°F/180–190°C, or until a cube of bread browns in 30 seconds.

Meanwhile, put the flour, sugar, salt, and baking powder in a medium–large bowl. Stir to combine the ingredients.

Make a well in the center and add the eggs and coconut milk. Whisk, gradually incorporating the dry ingredients into the wet ingredients, until the batter is smooth.

Add the bananas to the batter, making sure they are coated evenly all over.

Working in batches, lower the bananas into the hot oil and deep-fry for 5–7 minutes, or until golden and crispy.

Drain the bananas on a plate lined with paper towels.

Transfer to plates and serve, dusted with confectioners' sugar.

almond cookies

makes about 50 pieces

ingredients

generous 5⅓ cups all-purpose
 flour
½ tsp baking powder

½ tsp salt
generous ¾ cup slivered
 almonds
generous 1 cup diced lard

generous 1 cup granulated
 sugar
1 egg, lightly beaten
1½ tsp almond extract

50 whole almonds, to decorate
 (optional)

1 Preheat the oven to 325°F/160°C and line several cookie sheets with parchment paper. Sift the flour, baking powder, and salt together and set aside.

2 Pulverize the almond slivers in a food processor, add the flour mixture, and pulse until the nuts are well mixed with the flour.

3 Turn the flour-and-nut mixture into a large bowl, add the lard, and work into the flour until crumbly.

4 Add the sugar, egg, and almond extract and mix well until the dough is soft and pliable but still firm enough to be handled.

197

×5 Divide the dough into 1-inch/2.5-cm balls. Place on the lined cookie sheets 2 inches/5 cm apart, and flatten with the back of a spoon.

×6 Press a whole almond (if using) onto each cookie. Bake for 15–18 minutes.

Transfer to a wire rack to cool and serve.

mango with sticky rice squares

serves 4

ingredients
1 cup jasmine rice
generous 1 cup canned
  coconut milk
generous 1 cup water
scant ½ cup caster sugar
2 ripe mangoes
juice of 1 lime
shreds of lime zest, to decorate

>1 Grease an 8-inch/20-cm square pan. Place
the rice in a pan with the coconut milk,
water, and sugar and bring to a boil.

>2 Reduce the heat, cover, and simmer
for 20–25 minutes, stirring occasionally,
until tender and sticky.

Serve the rice squares with slices of mango, drizzled with puree and sprinkled with shreds of lime.

3 Spread the rice in the greased pan and let set. Cut into 4 squares when set.

>4 Peel, pit, and slice the mangoes and sprinkle with lime juice. Reserve a few slices and puree the rest in a food processor.

malaysian milk pudding

serves 4

ingredients

1½ oz/40 g vermicelli rice
 noodles
3 tbsp butter

3 cups milk
½ cup coconut cream
2 tbsp superfine sugar
1 cinnamon stick

3 cardamom pods
¼ cup golden raisins
½ tsp almond extract

pinch of ground turmeric
2 tbsp slivered almonds

1 Break the noodles into 2-inch/5-cm lengths.

2 Heat 2 tablespoons of the butter in a large pan and fry the noodles, stirring, until pale golden.

3 Add the milk, coconut cream, sugar, cinnamon, and cardamom and stir until almost boiling.

4 Reduce the heat, cover, and simmer for 10–12 minutes, stirring occasionally.

Add the golden raisins, almond extract, and turmeric and simmer for 5 minutes. Cool.

Fry the almonds in the remaining butter until golden.

Transfer to bowls, sprinkle with almonds, and serve.

oriental fruit salad

serves 4–6

ingredients

1 lime
2 lemon grass stalks, bruised
¼ cup superfine sugar
generous ⅓ cup boiling water

1 wedge watermelon, about
 14 oz/400 g in weight
half a Galia melon, about
 12 oz/350 g in weight
1 dragon fruit

1 star fruit (carambola)
sprigs of mint, to decorate
coconut ice cream, to serve
 (optional)

1 Pare a thin strip of rind from the lime and place in a heatproof pitcher or measuring cup with the lemon grass and sugar.

>2 Pour over the boiling water, stir to dissolve the sugar, then let completely cool.

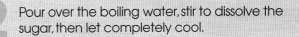

3 Peel and seed the melons and chop these and the dragon fruit into bite-size chunks.

>4 Trim the star fruit and cut into thin slices.

>5 Combine all the fruits in a wide bowl and squeeze over the juice of the lime.

>6 Strain the lemon grass syrup, pour over the fruit, and stir lightly.

Transfer to bowls, sprinkle with mint, and serve with ice cream, if using.

baked passion fruit custards

serves 4

ingredients
4 passion fruit
4 large eggs
¾ cup canned coconut milk
¼ cup superfine sugar
1 tsp orange flower water

>1 Preheat the oven to 350°F/180°C. Halve
3 passion fruit, scoop out the flesh, and rub
through a strainer to remove the seeds.

>2 Beat together the eggs, passion
fruit juice, coconut milk, sugar, and
orange flower water until smooth.

Serve the custards slightly warm or chilled.

> **3** Pour the custard into four 1-cup ovenproof dishes, place in a baking pan, and pour in hot water to reach halfway up the dishes.

> **4** Bake in the oven for 40–45 minutes, or until just set. Scoop the pulp from the remaining passion fruit and spoon a little onto each dish to serve.

toffee sweet potatoes

serves 4

ingredients

1 lb/450 g sweet potatoes,
  scrubbed
peanut oil, for frying

¾ cup sugar
1 tsp soy sauce
5 tbsp water
2 tsp sesame seeds

1. Cut the potatoes into ½ inch/1 cm thick slices, leaving the peel on.

>2 Cut each slice crosswise to make four wedges.

>3 Heat oil that is 1-inch/2.5-cm deep in a wok to 350–375°F/180–190°C, or until a cube of bread browns in 30 seconds. Fry the potatoes in batches for 2–3 minutes, until golden.

>4 Remove with a slotted spoon and drain on absorbent paper towels.

>5 Place the sugar, soy sauce, and water in a pan and stir on a low heat until the sugar dissolves.

>6 Boil the mixture until it becomes syrupy and darkens to a rich toffee color. Remove from the heat.

>7 Quickly toss the pieces of potato in the toffee, turning to coat evenly.

>8 Lift onto wax paper and sprinkle with sesame seeds. Let cool.

Serve the toffee potatoes immediately.

burmese semolina cake

serves 4

ingredients

½ cup butter
1½ cups coarse semolina
1¾ cups canned coconut
  milk

1¾ cups water
¾ cup light brown sugar
½ tsp ground cardamom
4 eggs, beaten
⅓ cup golden raisins

2 tbsp white poppy seeds or
sesame seeds

Preheat the oven to 400°F/200°C. Grease a 9-inch/23-cm square cake pan with 1 tablespoon of the butter.

>2 Place the semolina in a heavy-bottom pan and toast on a high heat, stirring until pale golden.

>3 Stir in the coconut milk, water, and sugar, then simmer, stirring constantly, until thickened.

>4 Remove from the heat and beat in the remaining butter, cardamom, eggs, and golden raisins.

Spread the mixture into the pan and
sprinkle with the poppy seeds.

>6 Bake for 40–45 minutes, until firm and
golden. Cool in the pan, then cut into
squares or diamond shapes.

Serve the cake cold as a snack, or warm
with fresh fruit for dessert.

sweet wontons

serves 4

ingredients
1 banana
½ cup pitted dates
⅓ cup blanched almonds
½ tsp ground cinnamon
20 wonton wrappers
1 egg white, lightly beaten
peanut oil, for deep-frying
confectioners' sugar, for dusting

>1 Peel the banana. Coarsley chop the dates, banana, and almonds, then mix with the cinnamon.

>2 Place 1 teaspoon of the fruit mixture in the center of each wonton wrapper.

Serve the wontons hot, lightly dusted with confectioners' sugar.

> **3** Brush the edges of the wonton with egg white, pull up the sides, then pinch together to seal. Pull out the corners.

> **4** Heat enough oil for deep-frying in a wok or large pan to 350-370°F/180-190°C, or until a cube of bread browns in 30 seconds. Deep-fry the wontons for 1–2 minutes, turning occasionally, until golden. Drain on paper towels.

Index